all-time
chris~~tmas~~
favourites
arranged for ukulele

Wise Publications
part of The Music Sales Group
London / New York / Paris / Sydney / Copenhagen / Berlin / Madrid / Tokyo

Published by:
Wise Publications,
14-15 Berners Street, London W1T 3LJ, UK.

Exclusive Distributors:
Music Sales Limited,
Distribution Centre, Newmarket Road, Bury St Edmunds,
Suffolk IP33 3YB, UK.
Music Sales Pty Limited,
20 Resolution Drive, Caringbah, NSW 2229, Australia.

Order No. AM995203
ISBN 978-1-84772-701-5
This book © Copyright 2008 Wise Publications,
a division of Music Sales Limited.

Edited by David Harrison.
Cover designed by Fresh Lemon.
Photographs courtesy of Matthew Ward.

Printed in the EU.

Your Guarantee of Quality
As publishers, we strive to produce every book to the highest
commercial standards.

The music has been freshly engraved and the book has been carefully designed
to minimise awkward page turns and to make playing from it a real pleasure.

Particular care has been given to specifying acid-free, neutral-sized
paper made from pulps which have not been elemental chlorine bleached.

This pulp is from farmed sustainable forests and was produced with
special regard for the environment.

Throughout, the printing and binding have been planned to ensure
a sturdy, attractive publication which should give years of enjoyment.

If your copy fails to meet our high standards, please inform us
and we will gladly replace it.

www.musicsales.com

all i want for christmas is you

Words & Music by Mariah Carey & Walter Afanasieff

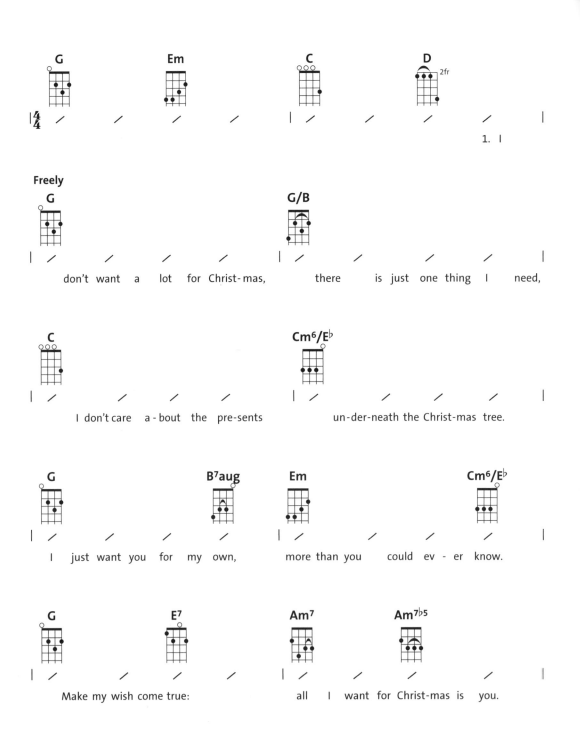

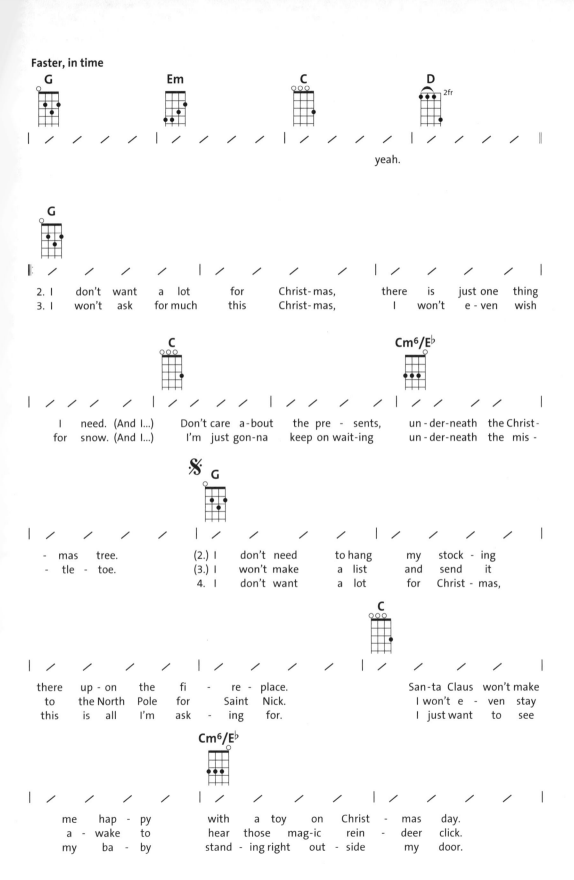

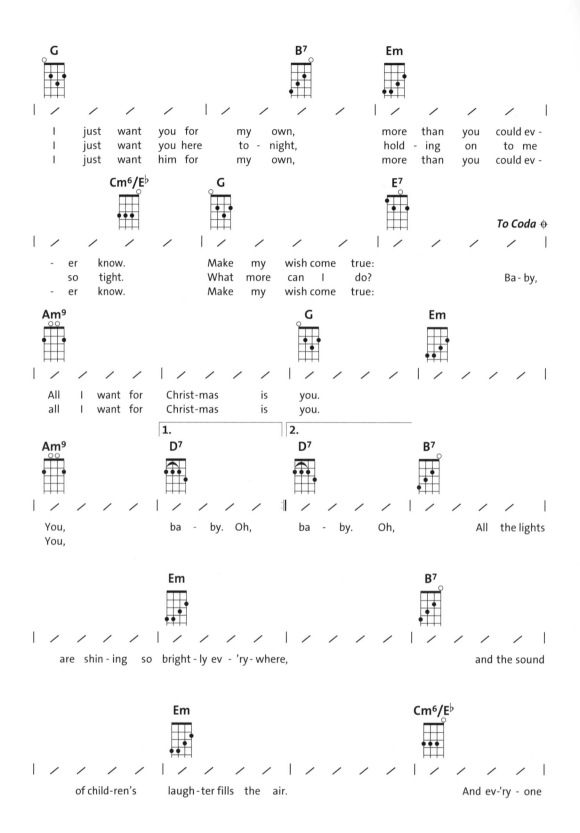

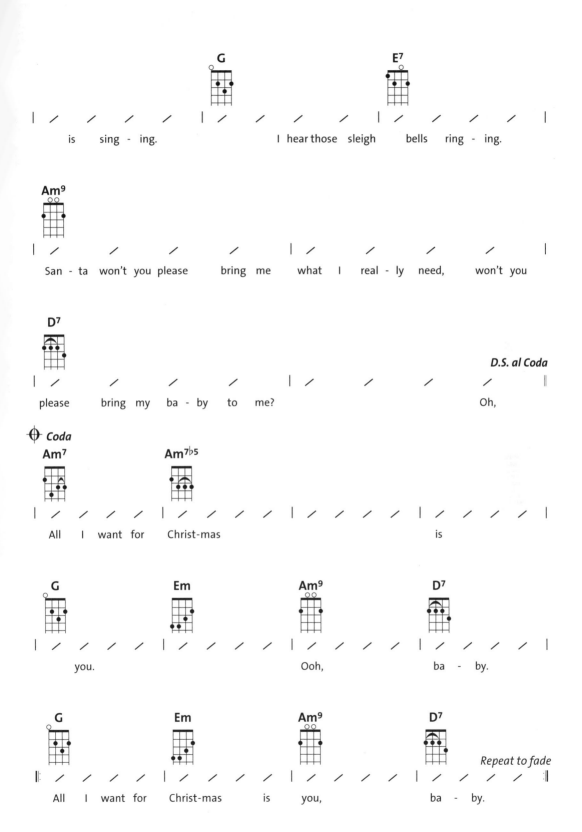

baby, it's cold outside

Words & Music by Frank Loesser

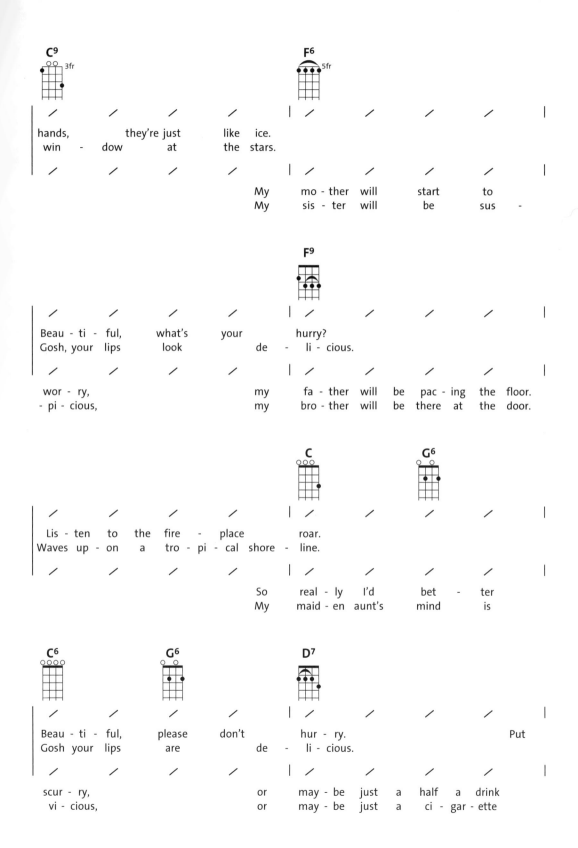

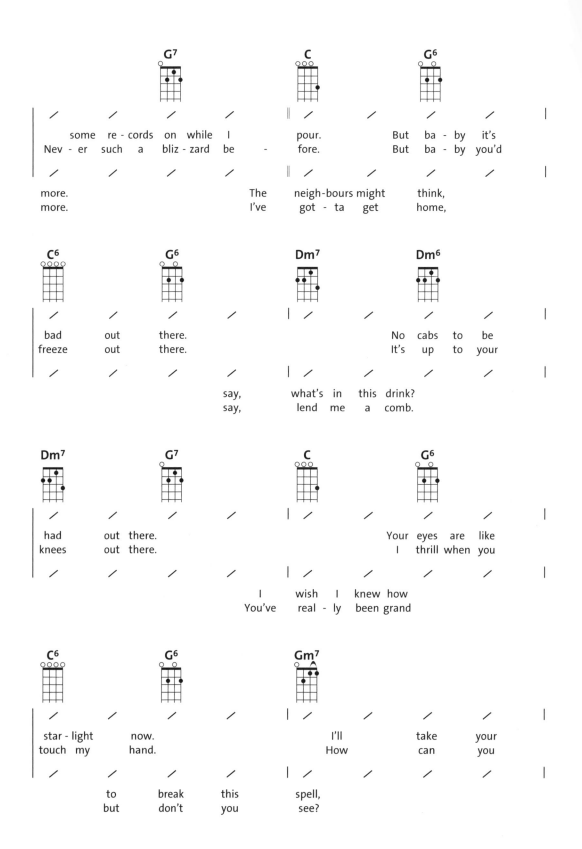

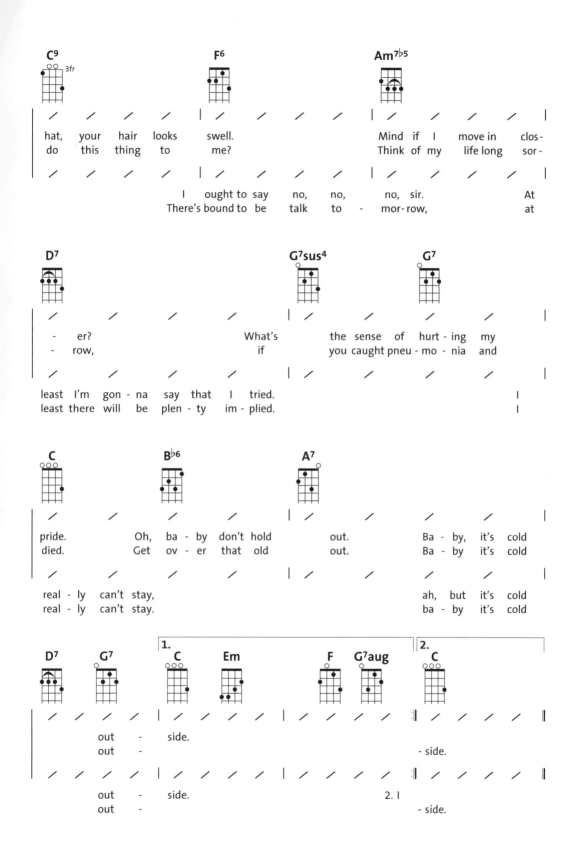

blue christmas

Words & Music by Billy Hayes & Jay Johnson

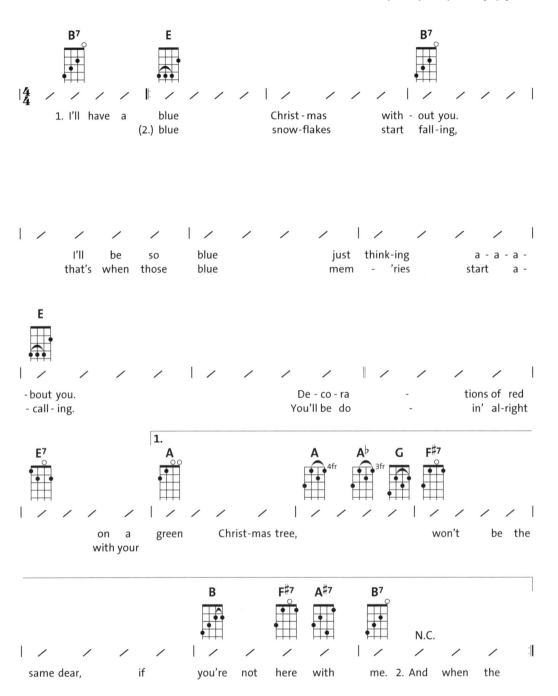

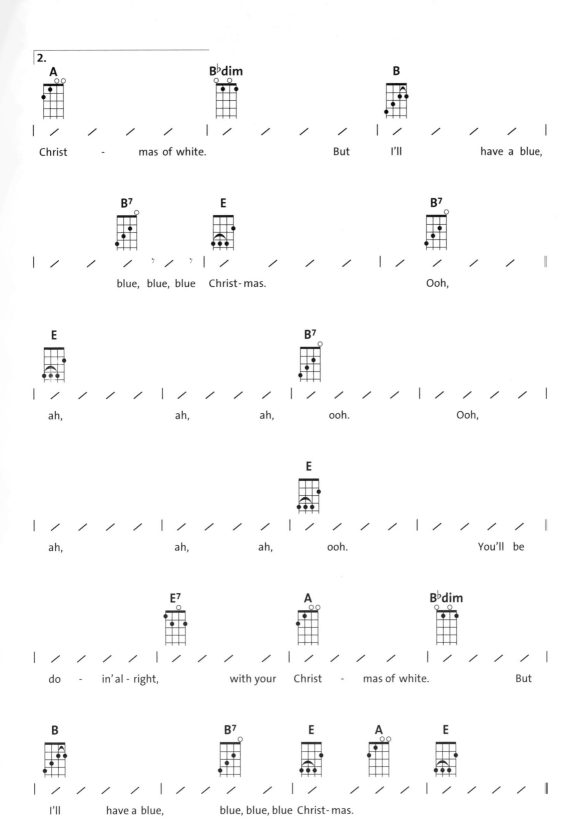

2.

A   B♭dim   B

Christ - mas of white.   But   I'll   have a blue,

B⁷   E   B⁷

blue, blue, blue   Christ-mas.   Ooh,

E   B⁷

ah,   ah,   ah,   ooh.   Ooh,

E

ah,   ah,   ah,   ooh.   You'll be

E⁷   A   B♭dim

do - in' al - right,   with your   Christ - mas of white.   But

B   B⁷   E   A   E

I'll   have a blue,   blue, blue, blue Christ-mas.

deck the halls

Traditional

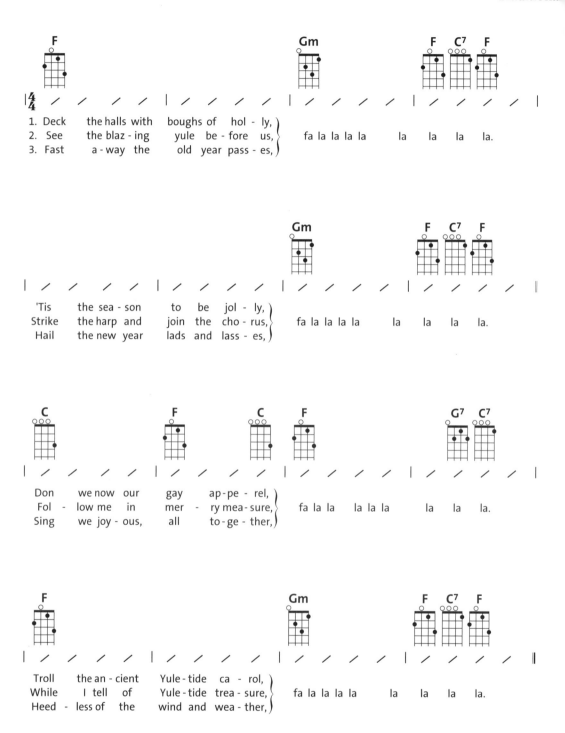

fairytale of new york

Words & Music by Shane MacGowan & Jem Finer

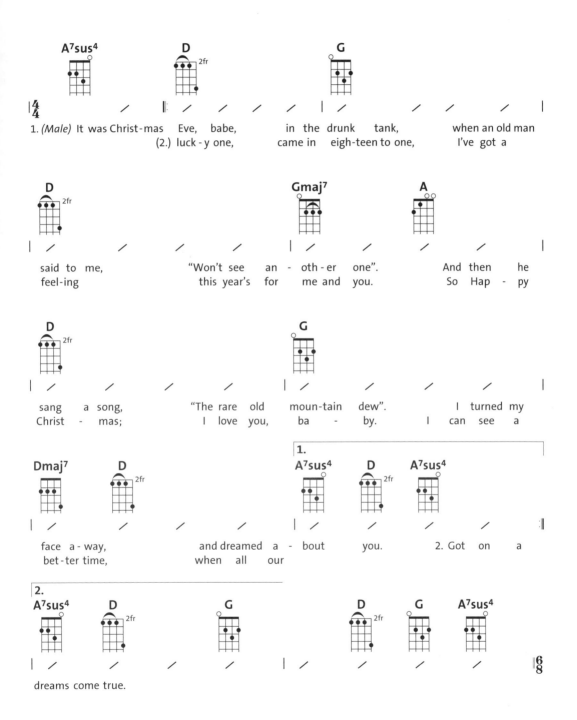

1. *(Male)* It was Christ-mas Eve, babe, in the drunk tank, when an old man
(2.) luck-y one, came in eigh-teen to one, I've got a

said to me, "Won't see an-oth-er one". And then he
feel-ing this year's for me and you. So Hap-py

sang a song, "The rare old moun-tain dew". I turned my
Christ-mas; I love you, ba-by. I can see a

1.
face a-way, and dreamed a-bout you. 2. Got on a
bet-ter time, when all our

2.
dreams come true.

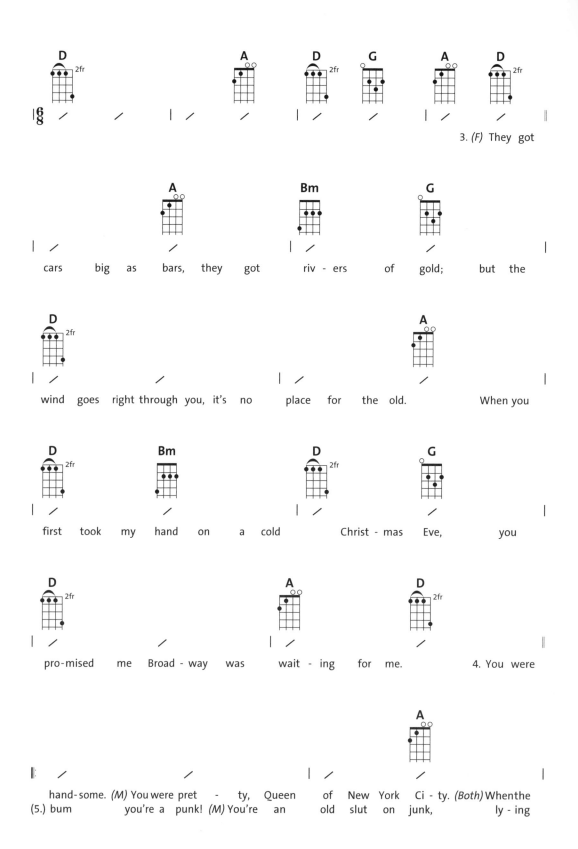

D 2fr   **A**   **D** 2fr   **G**   **A**   **D** 2fr

3. *(F)* They got

A   **Bm**   **G**

cars   big   as   bars,   they   got   riv - ers   of   gold;   but the

D 2fr   **A**

wind   goes   right through   you,   it's   no   place   for   the   old.   When you

D 2fr   **Bm**   **D** 2fr   **G**

first   took   my   hand   on   a   cold   Christ - mas   Eve,   you

D 2fr   **A**   **D** 2fr

pro-mised   me   Broad - way   was   wait - ing   for   me.   4. You were

A

hand-some. *(M)* You were pret - ty,   Queen   of   New   York   Ci - ty. *(Both)* When the
(5.) bum   you're a   punk! *(M)* You're   an   old   slut   on   junk,   ly - ing

16

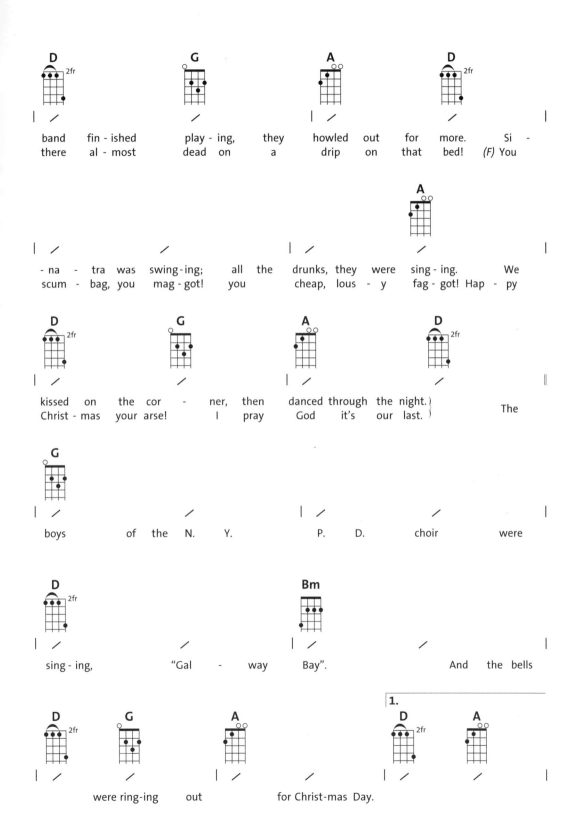

band   fin - ished   play - ing,   they   howled   out   for   more.   Si -
there   al - most   dead   on   a   drip   on   that   bed!   *(F)* You

- na - tra was   swing - ing;   all   the   drunks, they   were   sing - ing.   We
scum - bag, you   mag - got!   you   cheap, lous - y   fag - got! Hap - py

kissed   on   the   cor   -   ner,   then   danced through   the night.   The
Christ - mas   your arse!   I   pray   God   it's   our   last.

boys   of   the   N.   Y.   P.   D.   choir   were

sing - ing,   "Gal   -   way   Bay".   And   the bells

1.

were ring-ing   out   for Christ-mas Day.

17

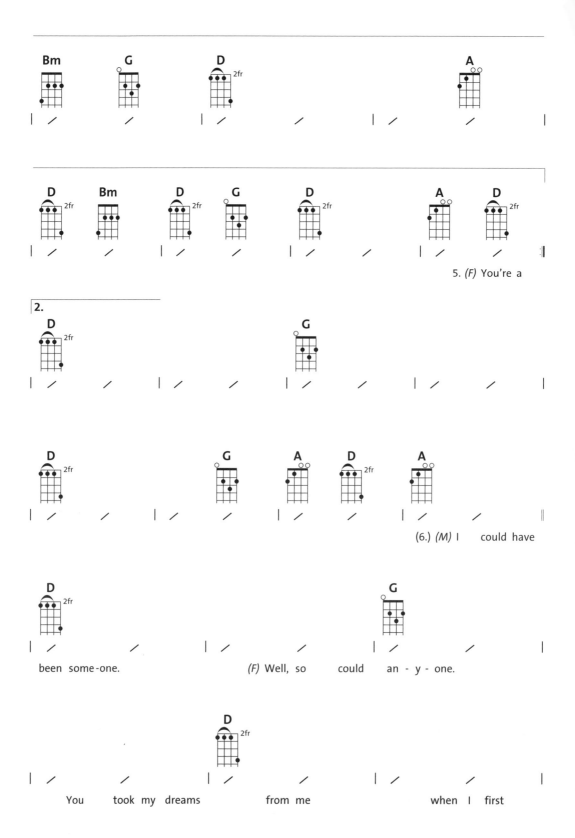

5. *(F)* You're a

(6.) *(M)* I   could have

been some-one.   *(F)* Well, so   could   an - y - one.

You   took my dreams   from me   when I first

18

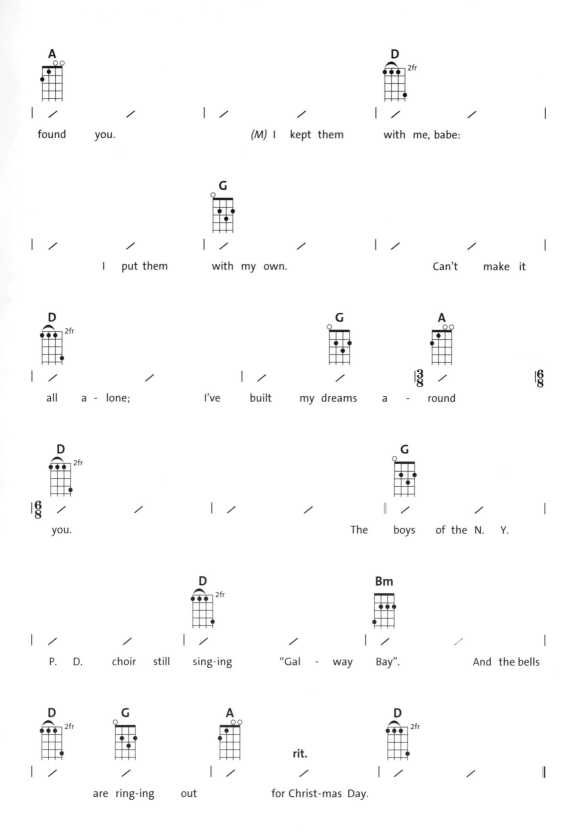

found you. *(M)* I kept them with me, babe:

I put them with my own. Can't make it

all a - lone; I've built my dreams a - round

you. The boys of the N. Y.

P. D. choir still sing-ing "Gal - way Bay". And the bells

rit.

are ring-ing out for Christ-mas Day.

god rest ye merry gentlemen

Traditional

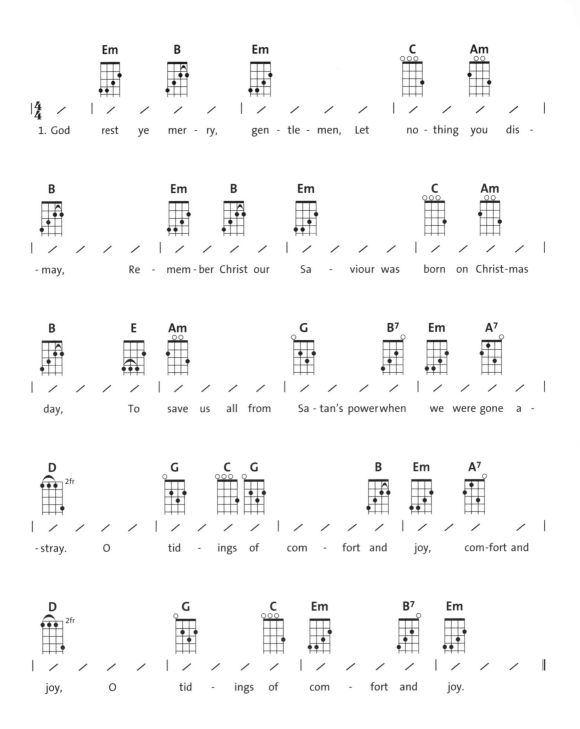

Verse 2:
From God our Heavenly Father
A blessed angel came,
And unto certain shepherds
Brought tidings of the same;
How that in Bethlehem was born
The Son of God by name.
   O tidings...

Verse 3:
"Fear not," then said the Angel,
"Let nothing you afright,
This day is born a Saviour
Of a pure Virgin bright,
To free all those that trust in Him
From Satan's power and might."
   O tidings...

Verse 4:
The shepherds at those tidings
Rejoiced much in mind,
And left their flock a-feeding,
In tempest, storm and wind;
And went to Bethlehem straightaway,
The Son of God to find.
   O tidings...

Verse 5:
Now to the Lord sing praises
All you within this place,
And with true love and brotherhood
Each other now embrace,
This holy tide of Christmas
All others do deface.
   O tidings...

happy xmas (war is over)

Words & Music by John Lennon & Yoko Ono

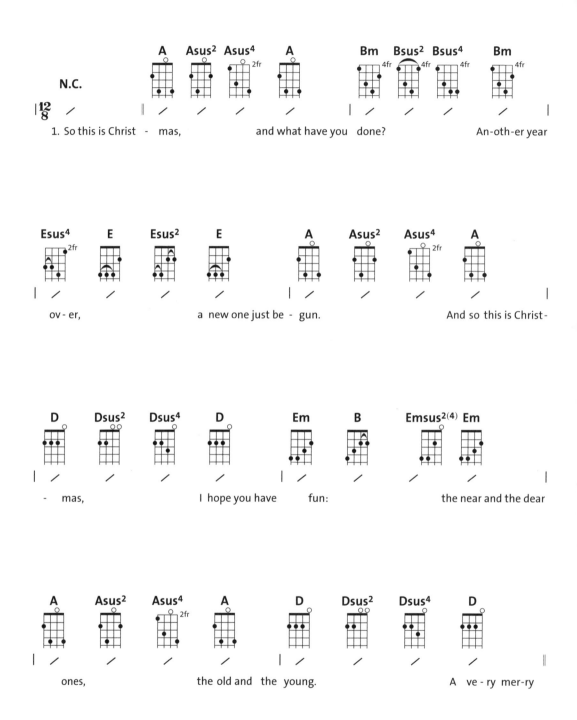

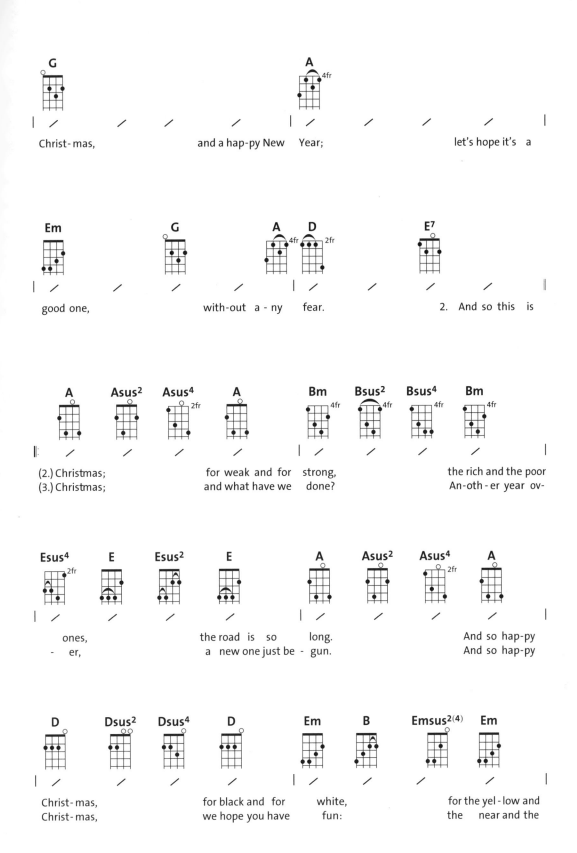

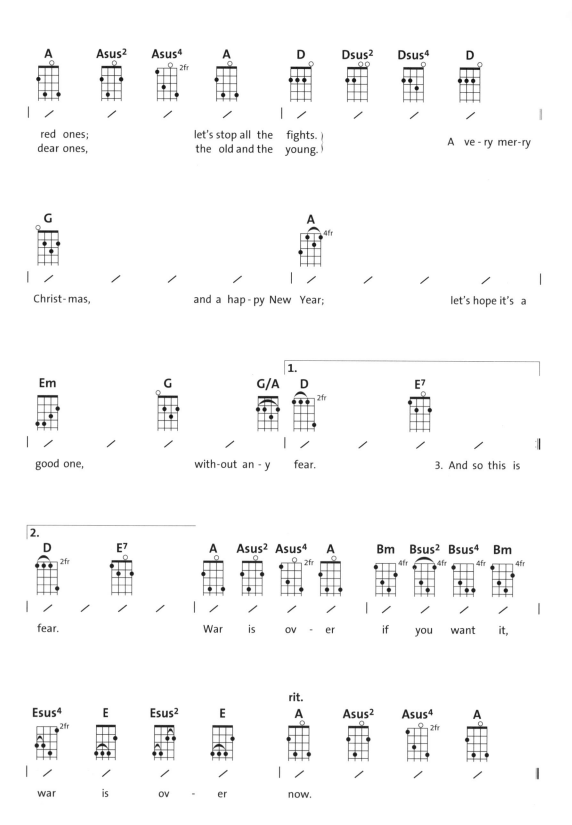

red ones;   let's stop all the   fights.
dear ones,   the old and the   young.

A ve - ry mer-ry

Christ-mas,   and a hap - py New   Year;

let's hope it's a

good one,   with-out an - y   fear.

3. And so this is

2.

fear.   War   is   ov - er   if   you   want   it,

rit.

war   is   ov - er   now.

24

jingle bells

Words & Music by J.S. Pierpont

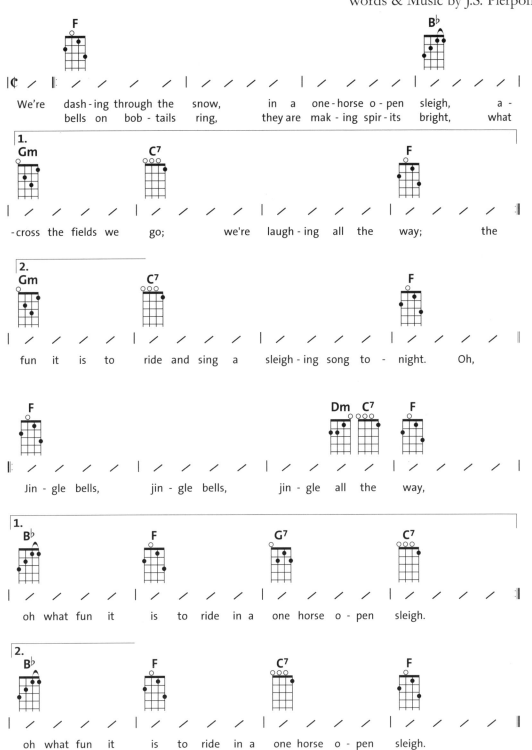

the holly and the ivy

Traditional

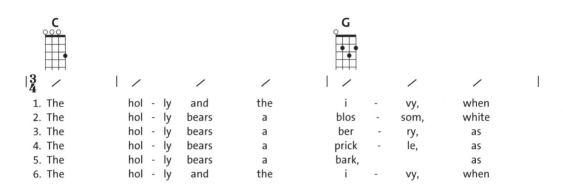

C				G			
1. The	hol - ly and	the	i - vy,	when
2. The	hol - ly bears	a	blos - som,	white
3. The	hol - ly bears	a	ber - ry,	as
4. The	hol - ly bears	a	prick - le,	as
5. The	hol - ly bears	a	bark,	as
6. The	hol - ly and	the	i - vy,	when

C		D	
they are both	full	grown,	of
as the lil - ly	flow'r,	and
red as a - ny	blood,	and
sharp as a - ny	thorn,	and
bit - ter as a - ny	gall,	and
they are both	full	grown,	of

Bm	Em	Bm	C	D
all the trees	that are	in the wood,	the
Ma - ry bore	sweet	Je - sus Christ,	to
Ma - ry bore	sweet	Je - sus Christ,	to
Ma - ry bore	sweet	Je - sus Christ,	on
Ma - ry bore	sweet	Je - sus Christ,	for
all the trees	that are	in the wood,	the

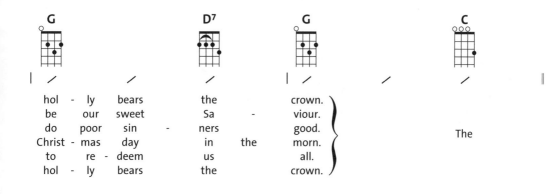

| G | | D⁷ | G | | C |

hol - ly bears the crown.
be our sweet Sa - viour.
do poor sin - ners good.
Christ - mas day in the morn.
to re - deem us all.
hol - ly bears the crown.

The

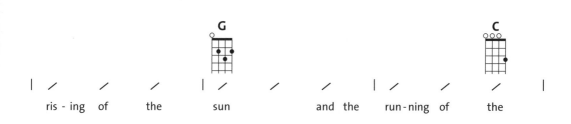

| | | | G | | | C |

ris - ing of the sun and the run - ning of the

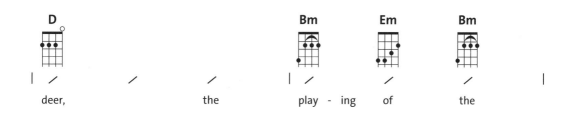

| D | | Bm | Em | Bm |

deer, the play - ing of the

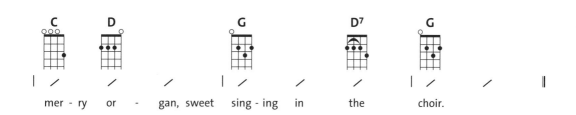

| C | D | G | D⁷ | G |

mer - ry or - gan, sweet sing - ing in the choir.

i saw three ships

Traditional

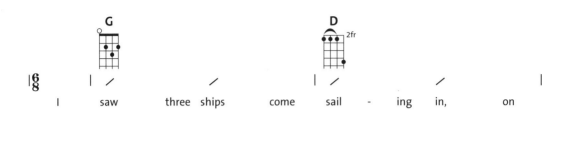

I saw three ships come sail - ing in, on

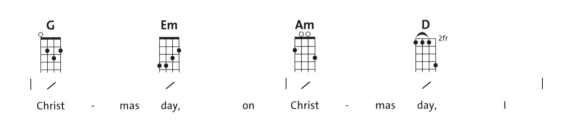

Christ - mas day, on Christ - mas day, I

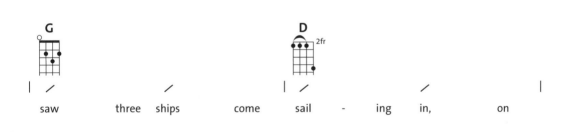

saw three ships come sail - ing in, on

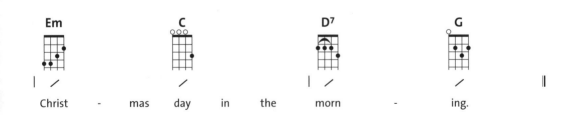

Christ - mas day in the morn - ing.

Verse 2:
And what was in those ships all three,
On Christmas Day, on Christmas Day?
And what was in those ships all three,
On Christmas Day in the morning?

Verse 3:
The Virgin Mary and Christ were there,
On Christmas Day, on Christmas Day;
The Virgin Mary and Christ were there,
On Christmas Day in the morning.

Verse 4:
Pray, wither sailed those ships all three,
On Christmas Day, on Christmas Day;
Pray, wither sailed those ships all three,
On Christmas Day in the morning?

Verse 5:
O they sailed into Bethlehem,
On Christmas Day, on Christmas Day;
O they sailed into Bethlehem,
On Christmas Day in the morning.

Verse 6:
And all the bells on earth shall ring,
On Christmas Day, on Christmas Day;
And all the bells on earth shall ring,
On Christmas Day in the morning.

Verse 7:
And all the Angels in Heaven shall sing,
On Christmas Day, on Christmas Day;
And all the Angels in Heaven shall sing,
On Christmas Day in the morning.

Verse 8:
And all the souls on earth shall sing,
On Christmas Day, on Christmas Day;
And all the souls on earth shall sing,
On Christmas Day in the morning.

Verse 9:
Then let us all rejoice again,
On Christmas Day, on Christmas Day;
Then let us all rejoice again,
On Christmas Day in the morning.

i wish it could be christmas every day

Words & Music by Roy Wood

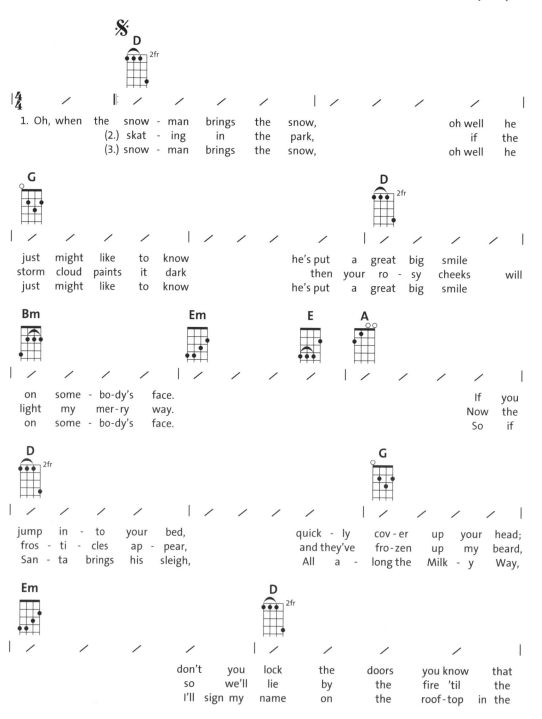

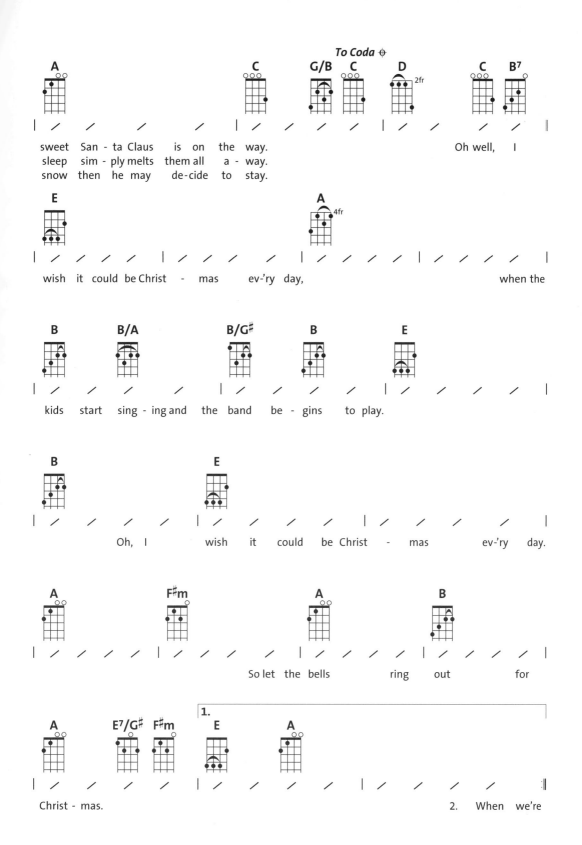

To Coda ⊕

A   C   G/B   C   D   C   B⁷

sweet San - ta Claus is on the way.   Oh well, I
sleep sim - ply melts them all a - way.
snow then he may de-cide to stay.

E   A

wish it could be Christ - mas ev-'ry day,   when the

B   B/A   B/G♯   B   E

kids start sing - ing and the band be - gins to play.

B   E

Oh, I wish it could be Christ - mas ev-'ry day.

A   F♯m   A   B

So let the bells ring out for

1.

A   E⁷/G♯ F♯m   E   A

Christ - mas.   2. When we're

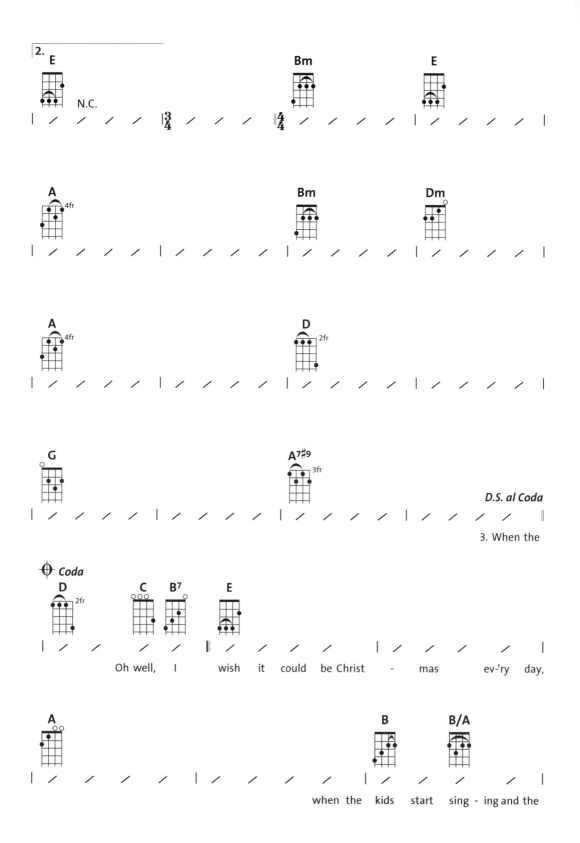

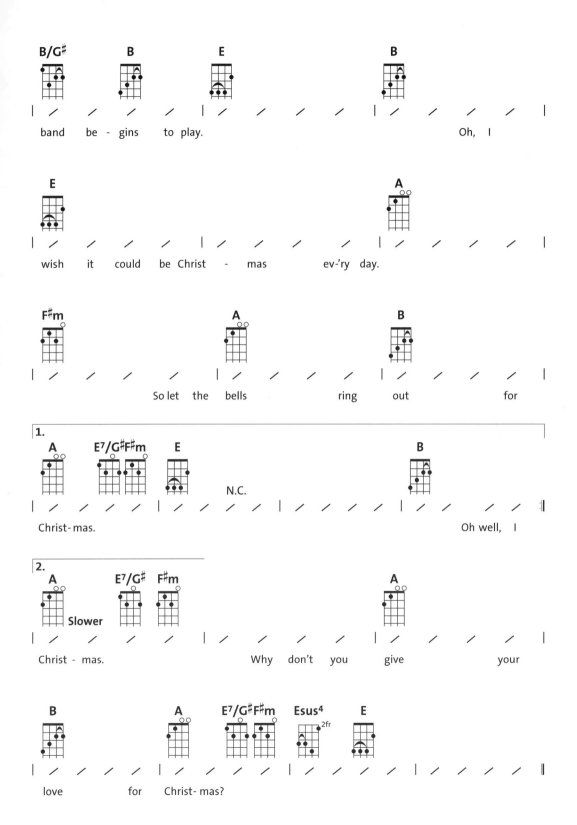

it's beginning to look like christmas

Words & Music by Meredith Willson

It's be - gin-ning to look a lot like Christ - mas,

ev - 'ry-where you go. Take a

look in the five - and -ten, glis -ten -ing once a -gain with

can - dy canes and sil - ver lanes a - glow. It's be -

- gin-ning to look a lot like Christ - mas,

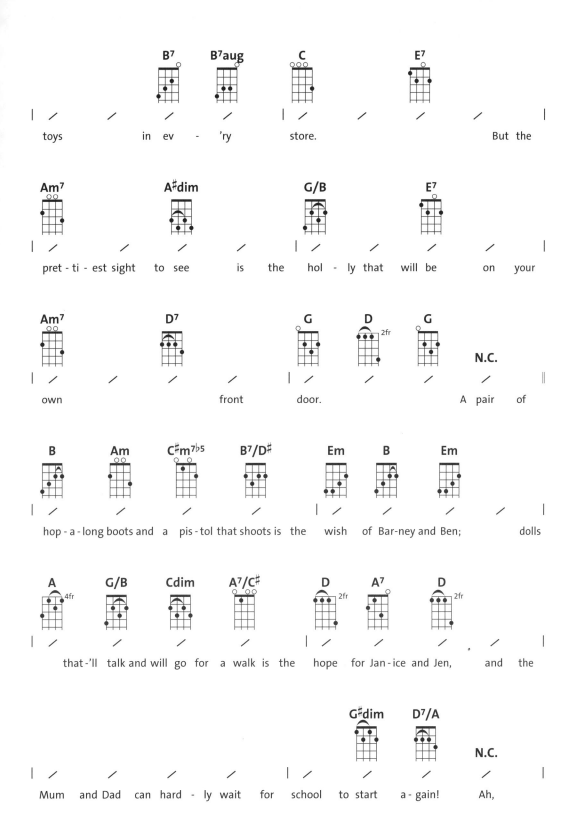

B7 B7aug C E7

toys in ev - 'ry store. But the

Am7 A#dim G/B E7

pret - ti - est sight to see is the hol - ly that will be on your

Am7 D7 G D G N.C.

own front door. A pair of

B Am C#m7b5 B7/D# Em B Em

hop - a - long boots and a pis - tol that shoots is the wish of Bar - ney and Ben; dolls

A G/B Cdim A7/C# D A7 D

that - 'll talk and will go for a walk is the hope for Jan - ice and Jen, and the

G#dim D7/A N.C.

Mum and Dad can hard - ly wait for school to start a - gain! Ah,

35

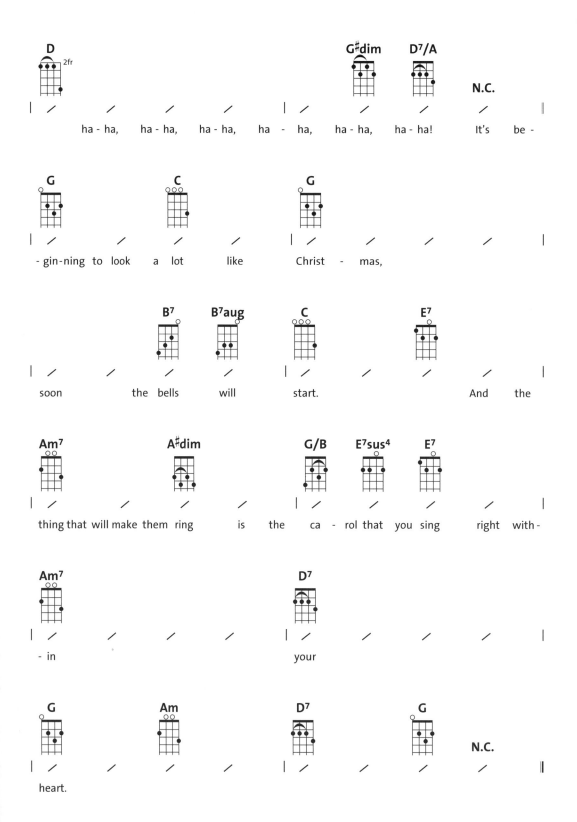

D 2fr   **G#dim**   **D7/A**   **N.C.**

ha - ha,   ha - ha,   ha - ha,   ha - ha,   ha - ha,   ha - ha!   It's   be -

G   **C**   **G**

- gin-ning to look   a   lot   like   Christ - mas,

B7   **B7aug**   **C**   **E7**

soon   the   bells   will   start.   And   the

Am7   **A#dim**   **G/B**   **E7sus4**   **E7**

thing that will make them ring   is   the   ca - rol that you sing   right   with -

Am7   **D7**

- in   your

G   **Am**   **D7**   **G**   **N.C.**

heart.

36

merry xmas everybody

Words & Music by Neville Holder & James Lea

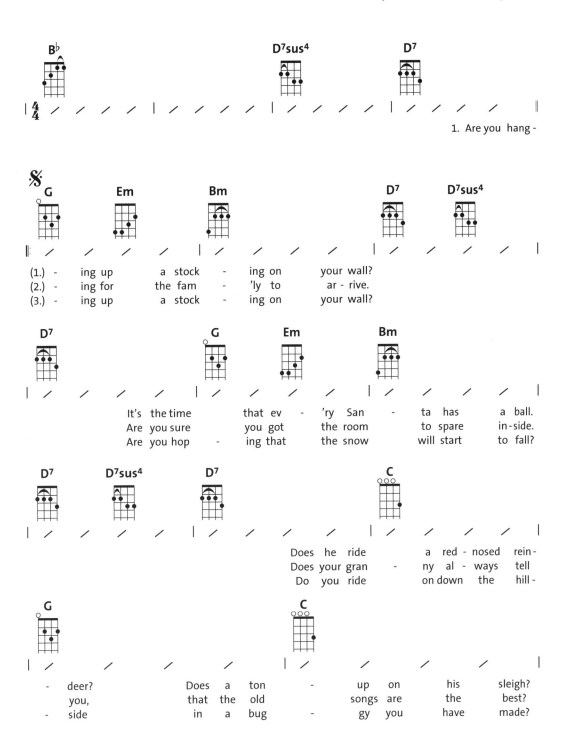

37

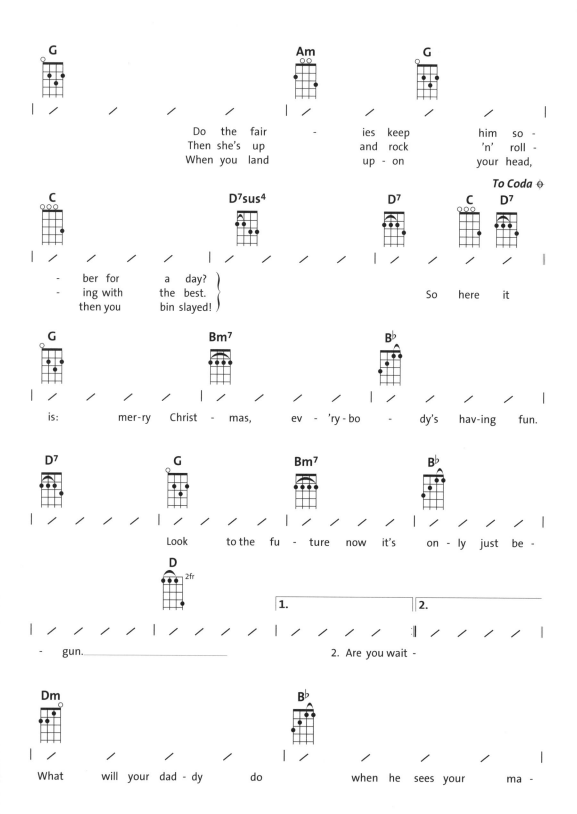

G   /   /   /   **Am**   /   /   **G**   /

Do the fair - ies keep him so -
Then she's up and rock 'n' roll -
When you land up - on your head,

To Coda ⊕

C   /   /   /   **D⁷sus⁴**   /   /   /   **D⁷**   /   /   **C**   **D⁷**   /

- ber for a day?
- ing with the best.   So here it
  then you bin slayed!

G   /   /   /   **Bm⁷**   /   /   /   **B♭**   /   /   /

is: mer-ry Christ - mas, ev - 'ry-bo - dy's hav-ing fun.

D⁷   /   /   /   **G**   /   /   /   **Bm⁷**   /   /   /   **B♭**   /   /   /

Look to the fu - ture now it's on - ly just be -

D 2fr

1.   **2.**

/   /   /   /   /   /   /   /   /   /   /

- gun._____   2. Are you wait -

Dm   /   /   /   **B♭**   /   /   /   /

What will your dad-dy do when he sees your ma -

38

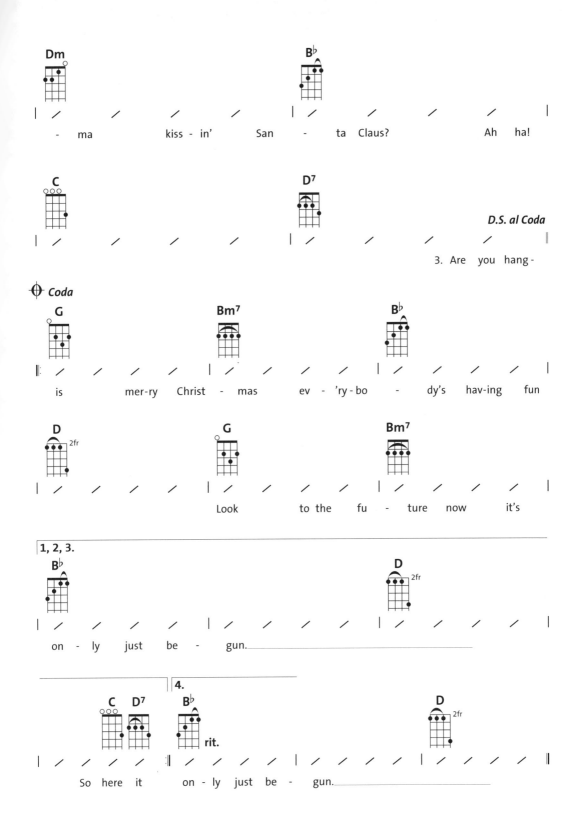

lonely this christmas

Words & Music by Mike Chapman & Nicky Chinn

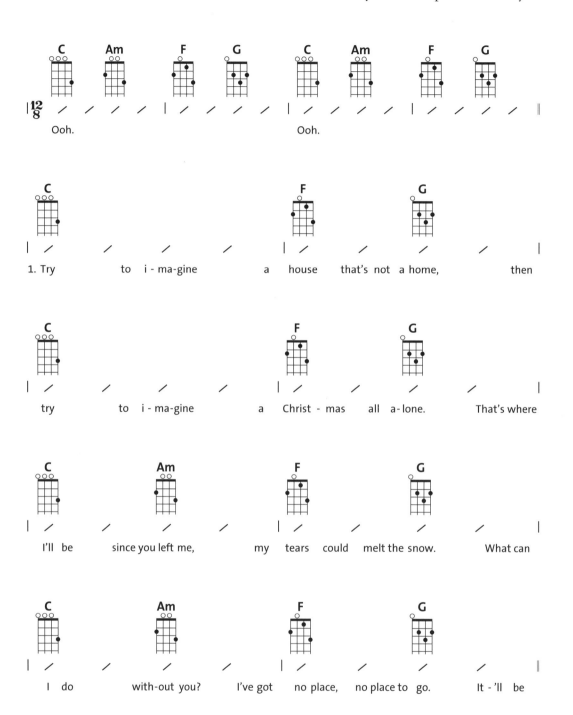

Ooh.   Ooh.

1. Try   to i - ma-gine   a   house   that's not a home,   then

try   to i - ma-gine   a   Christ - mas   all a-lone.   That's where

I'll be   since you left me,   my   tears   could   melt the snow.   What can

I   do   with-out you?   I've got   no place,   no place to go.   It - 'll be

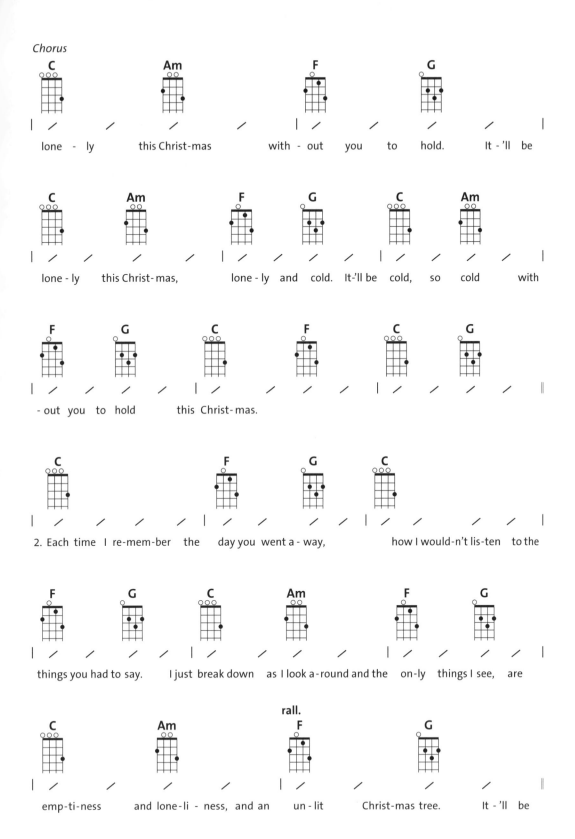

Chorus

C   Am   F   G

lone - ly   this Christ-mas   with - out   you   to   hold.   It -'ll be

C   Am   F   G   C   Am

lone - ly   this Christ-mas,   lone - ly and cold. It-'ll be   cold,   so   cold   with

F   G   C   F   C   G

- out   you   to   hold   this   Christ-mas.

C   F   G   C

2. Each time I re-mem-ber   the   day you went a - way,   how I would-n't lis-ten   to the

F   G   C   Am   F   G

things you had to say.   I just break down   as I look a-round and the   on-ly   things I see,   are

rall.

C   Am   F   G

emp-ti-ness   and lone-li - ness, and an   un - lit   Christ-mas tree.   It -'ll be

a tempo

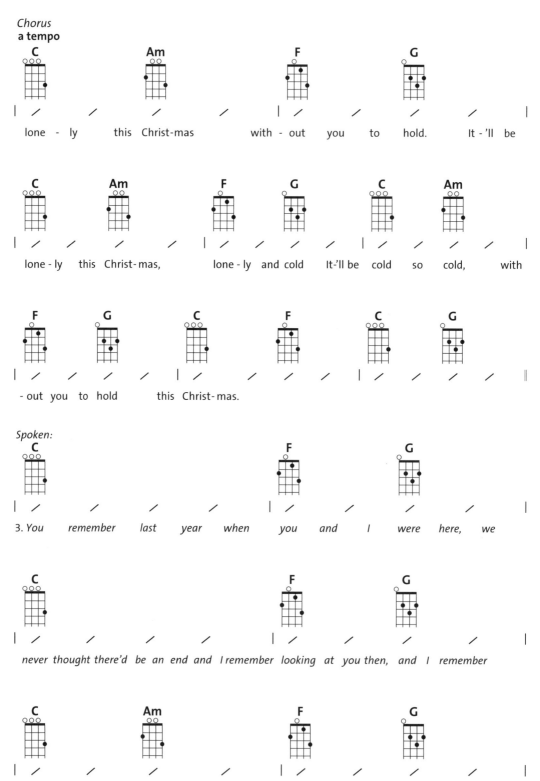

| C | Am | F | G |

lone - ly   this   Christ-mas   with - out   you   to   hold.   It - 'll   be

| C | Am | F | G | C | Am |

lone - ly   this Christ-mas,   lone - ly and cold   It-'ll be   cold   so   cold,   with

| F | G | C | F | C | G |

- out you to hold   this Christ-mas.

Spoken:

| C | F | G |

3. *You   remember   last   year   when   you   and   I   were   here,   we*

| C | F | G |

never thought there'd be an end and I remember looking at you then, and I remember

| C | Am | F | G |

thinking that Christmas, must have been made for us 'cause darling this is the time of year

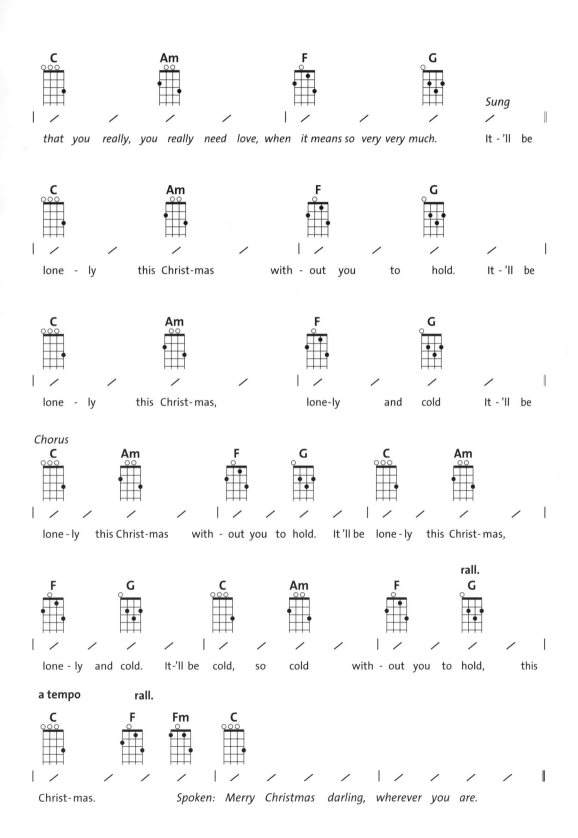

o christmas tree (o tannenbaum)

Traditional

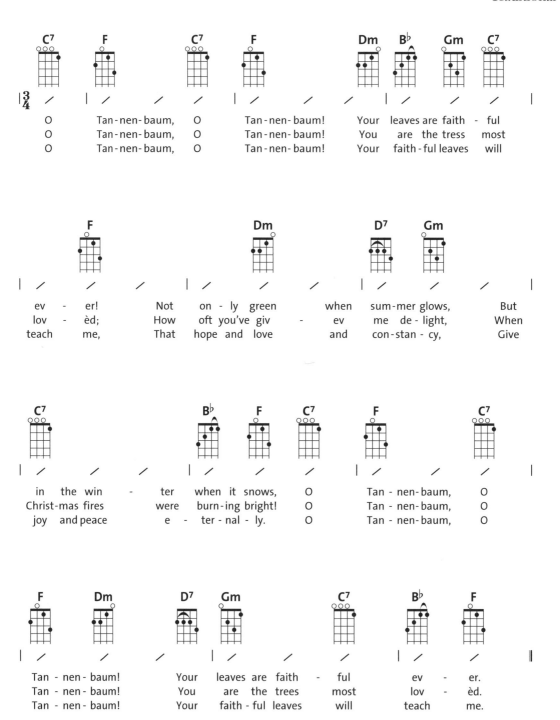

silent night

Words by Joseph Mohr
Music by Franz Gruber

the twelve days of christmas

Traditional

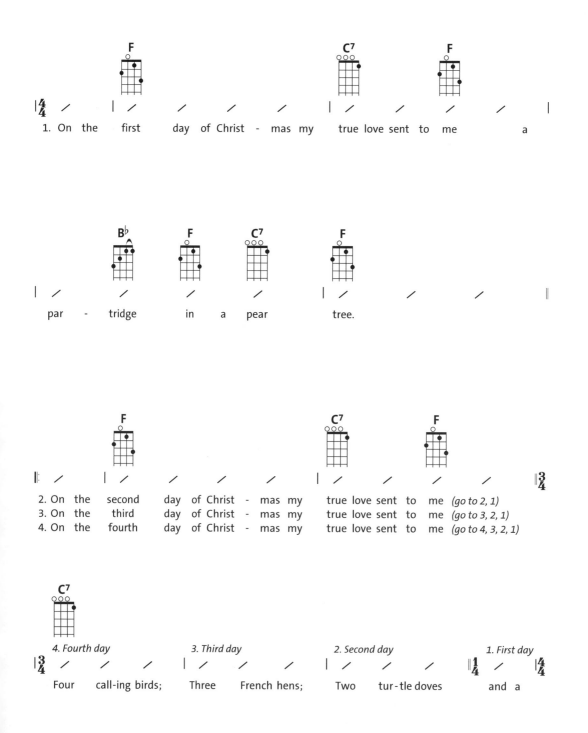

1. On the first day of Christ - mas my true love sent to me a

par - tridge in a pear tree.

2. On the second day of Christ - mas my true love sent to me *(go to 2, 1)*
3. On the third day of Christ - mas my true love sent to me *(go to 3, 2, 1)*
4. On the fourth day of Christ - mas my true love sent to me *(go to 4, 3, 2, 1)*

4. Fourth day *3. Third day* *2. Second day* *1. First day*

Four call-ing birds; Three French hens; Two tur-tle doves and a

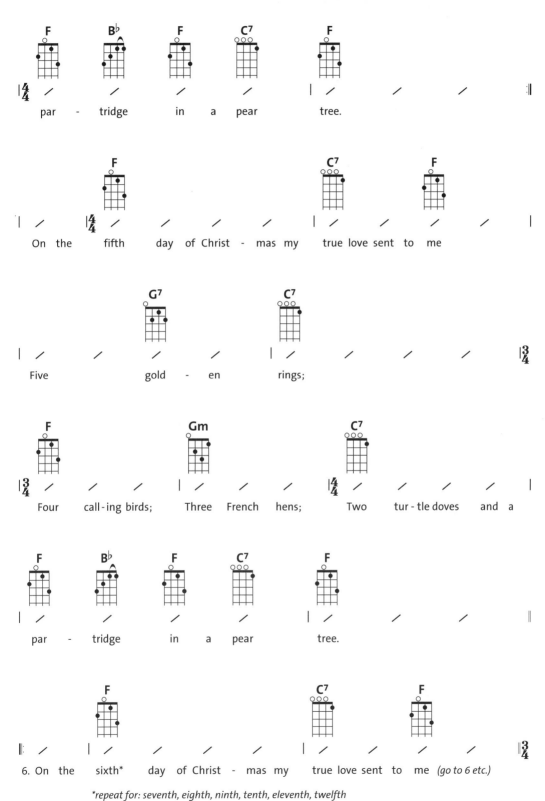

F   **B♭**   **F**   **C⁷**   **F**

| 4/4 /   /   /   / | /   /   /   :|

par - tridge   in   a   pear   tree.

F   **C⁷**   **F**

| / | 4/4 /   /   /   / | /   /   /   / |

On the   fifth   day of Christ - mas my   true love sent to   me

G⁷   **C⁷**

| /   /   /   / | /   /   /   / | 3/4

Five   gold - en   rings;

F   **Gm**   **C⁷**

| 3/4 /   /   / | /   /   / | 4/4 /   /   /   / |

Four   call-ing birds;   Three French hens;   Two   tur-tle doves   and   a

F   **B♭**   **F**   **C⁷**   **F**

| /   /   /   / | /   /   /   ‖

par - tridge   in   a   pear   tree.

F   **C⁷**   **F**

‖: / | /   /   /   / | /   /   /   / | 3/4

6. On the   sixth*   day of Christ - mas my   true love sent to   me *(go to 6 etc.)*

repeat for: seventh, eighth, ninth, tenth, eleventh, twelfth